Tiny Universe

Tiny Universe

Poems by

Rachel Beachy

© 2025 Rachel Beachy. All rights reserved.
This material may not be reproduced in any form, published,
reprinted, recorded, performed, broadcast,
rewritten or redistributed without
the explicit permission of Rachel Beachy.
All such actions are strictly prohibited by law.

Cover design by Shay Culligan
Cover image by Donny Jiang on Unsplash
Author photo by Patti Hartog

ISBN: 978-1-63980-778-9
Library of Congress Control Number: 2025943311

Kelsay Books
502 South 1040 East, A-119
American Fork, Utah 84003
Kelsaybooks.com

For my children.

Acknowledgments

Thank you to the following publications, in which versions of these poems previously appeared:

The Bluebird Word: "Swing"
Ephemera: "Object Impermanence," "The Butterfly Effect," "The Most Human Color," "These Years, These Days"
Eunoia Review: "Laws of Nature," "Baby Fever," "The Long Way Home," "What I Want to Tell My Daughter When She Falls Over and Over as She Learns to Walk," "The Orchid"
Freshwater Literary Journal: "Vigilant/e," "What I Remember of Pain"
Molecule: "Beach Body"
The Orchards Poetry Journal: "The First Trimester"
The Ravens Perch: "Saudade," "Ode to Mary Oliver"
The Rising Phoenix Review: "My Daughter's Hunger," "Little Thrills"
The Spearhead Magazine: "Doing My Best"
Steam Ticket: "Tiny Universe," "A Mutual Education"
Wildscape. Literary Journal: "The Night Is Dead, the Babies Are Alive, the Mothers Are Somewhere in Between"

Contents

Greetings	15
Baby Fever	16
The First Trimester	17
Ten Centimeters	18
An Infant's First Breath Inflates the Lungs, Dramatically Decreases Lung Pressure and Resistance to Blood Flow, Causing a Major Circulatory Reconfiguration	19
Afterpains	20
The Long Way Home	21
The Most Human Color	22
In/Out	23
My Daughter's Hunger	24
Diastasis Recti	25
What I Remember of Pain	26
Object Impermanence	27
The Night Is Dead, the Babies Are Alive, the Mothers Are Somewhere in Between	28
The Orchid	29
The Way Time Passes	30
Mother's Day as a Mother of Two	31
Baby Toes	32
Swing	33
Hysterical Strength	34
To a New Mother After a Long Night	35
Mother/Hero	36
I'm Sorry for the Things I Said When I Was Tired	37
A Mutual Education	38
This Means War	39
A Father Throws His Daughter in the Air	40
First Date (Postpartum)	41

The Night Is Dead, the Babies Are Alive, the Mothers Are Somewhere in Between (Part II)	42
Knots	43
Flu Season	44
There There	45
Homemaker	46
Vigilant/e	48
Saudade	49
On a Cold Morning, Dreaming	50
These Are the (Snow) Days	52
A Mutual Education (Part II)	53
Little Thrills	54
When Someone Tells Me the Days Are Long	55
Questions Before Becoming a Mother	56
Mycorrhizal Network	57
Natural Light	58
These Years, These Days	60
Cautionary Tales	61
What I Want to Tell My Daughter When She Falls Over and Over as She Learns to Walk	63
The Way With Children	64
Ode to Mary Oliver	65
Happy (and She Knows It)	66
Car Nap	67
Looking at Her Looking at Me	68
I'll Be Down Soon	69
The Butterfly Effect	70
Laundry List	71
To My Secondborn	72
Idea	73

A Mom on Social Media	74
Beach Body	76
My Daughter's Hunger (Part II)	77
Laws of Nature	78
Spoilers	79
To a Dear Friend	80
Tiny Universe	81
Mindfulness	82
Instructions for Calming Down	84
Doing My Best	85
Core Memory	86
As for Me and My House	87
Soundtrack	88
Little Shoes	89
Buckling My Toddler Into Her Car Seat	90
When the News Is Terrible Again	91
A Magic Trick	92
While You Are Reading This	93
This Never Gets Old	94
If the World Ended Tomorrow	96

Notes

*Look, I say, there is the sun, the grass, the fresh air
—all this you will take for granted someday
and then rediscover with a baby in your arms.*

—Weike Wang

Greetings

I hope this finds you
nap trapped / cluster feeding / in the witch-
ing hour / hiding behind the curtains from a
toddler who can't count to ten / taking deep
breaths / on a park bench covered in crumbs /
running late / in awe as the train goes by /
holding hands, pinky wrapped around her
wrist / waiting in the carpool line / picking
up Duplos / and pieces of yourself every night
putting back together a woman who loves so
                                              well.

Baby Fever

Someday she will ask
how I knew I was ready
and this is what I will tell her:
I had the feeling of someone
I could no longer wait to meet.
The person was you,
and it was me with you.
For all of the things I wasn't sure of
(such as how to be a mother)
I believed in us completely.

The First Trimester

Tell me something
good and true
like how a group of hummingbirds
is called a shimmer
or charm
and fragile wings
are meant to fly
tell me again
how the tiniest hearts
go on beating.

Ten Centimeters

When it happens it will come
from that other place
everything and nothing
has prepared you for this—
the most natural/unnatural
thing in the world
you want to die
the only thing you want more
is not to die
so you pull
the deepest part of yourself
from the molten core
bring her forth
break in two
and keep living.

An Infant's First Breath Inflates the Lungs, Dramatically Decreases Lung Pressure and Resistance to Blood Flow, Causing a Major Circulatory Reconfiguration

With a single breath
two hearts
will never be
the same.

Afterpains

The first time I held her there was pain
as the place where she just was
got smaller
as if to remind me
       there is no going back
and nothing lasts
not this or
            what comes next
all I can do is hold each moment
with gentle hands.

The Long Way Home

Everything changed
when you were born
we did not even take
the same route home
your father looked up
back roads and drove
so slowly while you slept
I was next to you in a
new world, dreaming
with my eyes wide open.

The Most Human Color

How easy it is
to lose track of each other
in this life
and yet
we only just met
and when I so much as
walk across the room
away from her
she cries
like I might never come back
I'm telling you
her face turns
blue.

In/Out

When I hold my baby
we are not two people
trying to get comfortable
there is no negotiating
of limbs and bones
no sharp angles
or strain
there is only
her cheek to my chest
my hand in her hair
and the way our bellies rise to meet
on the inhale.

My Daughter's Hunger

The baby's hunger
kept her (and me) awake
I had to admire the way
she just showed up
and refused to be denied.
The only thing I prayed for
more than sleep
was for her appetite to awaken
the whole world
someday.

Diastasis Recti

Nobody told the butterfly
to get its body back.
Nobody looked at the
soup-like substance of that caterpillar
as it dissolved in the cocoon—
triggered by hormones—
and lamented
things will never be the same.
We're metamorphosizing here!
And the places where we grow
are soft.

What I Remember of Pain

Not the contractions
the epidural
or the pushing
but the pinprick
where they drew blood
from my baby's heel.

Object Impermanence

I could not remember where I left
my phone or my coffee or
the rest of my sentence
there were burp cloths everywhere
but always out of reach
the swaddle that fit her the night before
was too small by the next morning
which is when I found a wine glass
on the bathroom counter
and my toothbrush
by the kitchen sink
next to the pacifiers
and bottles
and pump parts
that would need to be washed again that evening
and the next, and the next, and

The Night Is Dead, the Babies Are Alive, the Mothers Are Somewhere in Between

In the middle of the night
when you are awake with the baby
and everyone else is asleep
it is not nothing to know
robins start singing
when it's still dark
so certain are they
the sun will rise.

The Orchid

I do not remember the meal they brought
after the baby was born
I remember the orchid
which sat on my windowsill
for months afterward
as if to say, here
is something beautiful
to look at
and water if you feel like it
but if not?
Just wait and see—
it will still bloom as you go about
washing the bottles
picking up burp cloths
pacing the halls at night.
You might even think
(and you are not wrong
nor are you right)
it is blooming for you.

The Way Time Passes

with the baby—
every time I carry her
down the stairs
I feel as if I am going to
miss a
        step.

Mother's Day as a Mother of Two

Do not stop
to buy flowers this year
or leave to go buy them on Saturday—
not even during naptime.
Just come home
stay home
let me be the one
to go.

Baby Toes

When I take the baby
for a walk in the stroller
a woman stops me
grabs her feet, says
>*Where are her shoes?*

When my husband takes the baby
for a walk in the stroller
a woman stops him
grabs her feet, says
>*Oh! I just love*
>*baby toes.*

Swing

Pushing her swing back and forth
with the baby on my chest
I do not know
the day the time or how
to finish a thought
all of the hours go into
something like this

returning to baseline
a pendulum swinging
from mess to order
hunger to fullness
chaos to calm, repeat
and all along
they are growing

I see it now—
her hands wrapped tightly
around the chains of the
big girl swing
she could not reach last week—
how I watch her fly forward and
go nowhere at all

these days
thank God
thank God
how they
always
come back
to me.

Hysterical Strength

It was not a car I lifted but my body,
broken by labor and months of broken sleep,
from bed in the dead of night
her cry the only sound
I could not sleep through
could seem like
the only one in the world
yet in a house down the street
another light was on.
This is not a front-page story
of life or death
but it should be
how over and over
we crossed the expanse of night
to save them
and every time we thought
we could not do it
we did.

To a New Mother After a Long Night

This is not to say
the days are long but the years are short
you've got your hands full
or
they're only this little once

I am not here to tell you
this is your highest calling
cherish every moment
or
just wait until (fill in the blank)

What I want to be true:
it takes a village
when so often
the village is asleep
when you need them the most

This is just to say
I hope the next time
you make it out of the house
(and you will make it out again
someday, I promise)

someone smiles at your baby
and has the wisdom to know
what a new mother needs to hear
most of all
is quiet.

Mother/Hero

Just look at her go—
oh, but you should see the way
she stays.

I'm Sorry for the Things I Said
When I Was Tired

I meant to say, I am on your side. You make
the best coffee and the best babies. You're the
only other person who knows about the creak
in the floorboard outside the nursery and steps
over it. I am already counting down until you
get home. Nobody else can hold both children
and make it look so easy. Nobody else held my
hand the moment I became a mother. When I
can't sleep, it's not your fault, and when I can,
for however long we've got, I want to be
by your side.

A Mutual Education

There comes a time
to teach the baby
to fall asleep
on her own
to hold her until
her eyes nearly close
but not quite
and make way
for dreams to carry her
so it begins:
a lesson in letting go
at just the right moment.

This Means War

My baby just learned to wave—
it's one of three things
she knows how to do—
and when we walked by
that person did not wave back.

A Father Throws His Daughter in the Air

The world
and its problems
become smaller
for a moment
and she laughs
on
the
way
down
her joy in flying
is being caught.

First Date (Postpartum)

We go to dinner and call it a first date
like that one ten years ago that started it all
and when we leave the restaurant, he finds
an acorn in his pocket from one of the children
we tried not to talk about the whole time
we were gone, like they were with us
all along—what I mean is
maybe even back then.

The Night Is Dead, the Babies Are Alive, the Mothers Are Somewhere in Between (Part II)

In the middle of the night
when the baby is awake
and you are sleepwalking
with her in your arms
it is not nothing to know
someone once did this for you.

Knots

When my mother was away
I was busy being a mother
trying to teach my child
how to crawl
but still, I missed her
even the knot at the end
of my favorite necklace
reminded me of her
the way I pictured her hands
as I untangled it
and that love—
loosening the tension
and letting go
little by little
all those years—
where would I be without it?
I look at my child
and get down
on my hands and knees.

Flu Season

Dinner / the world / her forehead
is burning. Can we reschedule? Test
says negative. Not sure what to make
of the results. Still can't believe. Still
not sleeping. Maybe next week, or four
years from now. How are we going to
explain? Like a bad fever dream. She's
just waking—let me get back to you.
We'll find a time. We'll find a way
to get back to ourselves.

There There

It is not lost on me
that when we came to the place
where birdsong faded
I swore it had
our daughter learned
the perfect imitation of a crow
and everywhere we turned
she pointed to the trees and sky
as if to say there
        there.

Homemaker

I see the way you spend your day
returning to baseline—tears wiped /
crumbs swept / laundry washed / books
and puzzles put away—clean up, clean
up, everybody but mostly yourself doing
everyone's share. And if all goes well,
everything will be as it was when the day
began, then you will do it all over again
and again. But I promise this is not a zero-
sum. Look around. Your children are free
here, in a place they call their own, in this
place you have made
a home.

I see   you
returning to

                              yourself

                                       again
and
                    Your children
                         call
        you
     home

Vigilant/e

It starts and ends with a vigil

The hours I would have been asleep
now spent peering into her crib
watching for the smallest rise
and fall of her chest
preparing in me the vigilance it would take
once she started to crawl
        small, choke-able things
        suddenly everywhere
how blind I had been!
No longer
I was nothing
if not vigilant and so
I was a good mother

To keep young children alive—
this is good and necessary and
difficult work

I began to think of us all as vigilantes
how we did not trust the laws
of man or nature or
the universe itself
to do what we could
for these babies
these people
who would someday
should we do this well

keep vigil for us.

Saudade

My father comes over and brings
a pear for my daughter
perfectly ripe, so the juice
drips down her chin
as she sits on the kitchen counter
bare feet dangling.
All day afterward
she smells like fruit
sweet and slightly acidic
plus salt from so many tears
her face still sticky as she
presses against mine hours later
while I sing her to sleep.
And on the coldest day
I will think of this—
a single pear
and the love that remains
long after it is gone.

On a Cold Morning, Dreaming

The children are sleeping
and I am thinking
of the woman I used to be
the woman who would spend
cold mornings like this quietly
and could live each day
according to some kind of
plan called mine
not so anymore
when the children wake
a little bigger
than the night before
the dream now
for slowing down
and more time, of course,
the one thing
we cannot keep
still—to be the woman I am
when the woman I was
had been dreaming
of this very morning.

                        to

            live

        the

    dream
and
            keep

                dreaming

These Are the (Snow) Days

They wake and run to the window
see a perfect expanse of white
and ask if we can go outside
as soon as it gets light.
We pull on boots and mittens
puffy coats and hats as well
only to go outside for ten minutes
before someone says it's cold.
These days I can kiss their rosy cheeks
and make it all better
wipe their runny noses on my sleeve
and carry them up the hill over and over.
At the end of the day
I'm the one looking out the window
their tracks canvassing the snow
no longer a flawless blanket, and yet
this is my perfect view.

A Mutual Education
(Part II)

There is something to be said
for the way she signs for "more"
before she can say
any words—
before mama
before dada
there is longing
there is asking for it
with reckless abandon.

Little Thrills

Dropping off the kids with their grandparents /
coming home to an empty house / leaving the
baby gate open at the top of the stairs / losing
track of the monitor / and time / the moment
he walks in the door / dinner with no one on
my lap / or stealing bites / and easy conversation /
not even sweeping the floor afterward / the bed-
room door unlocked / and mouths uncovered /
waking to the sound of nothing / drinking coffee
while it is still hot / in mugs without lids / how
I miss them / how he says it first / and asks
when they'll be home.

When Someone Tells Me the Days Are Long

Thank goodness!
Give me
the longest day—
up before dawn
minutes dripping by
in some mind-numbing
repetition of
snacks
wiping snot
refereeing a lesson
in sharing,
a marathon just to
get out the door
only to stop and smell
every flower along the way—
because at the end of my life
I will never say
*if only the days
had been shorter.*

Questions Before Becoming a Mother

What if I can't do it?
What if everything I've heard is true? Or false?
What if I never sleep again?
What if I don't recognize myself?
What if it's not what I'm expecting?
What if it's even better?

Mycorrhizal Network

The pacifier we lost
on a trail in the woods
has been so carefully placed
on a tree stump
for us to find.
All at once
the baby is asleep
and I am not alone.

Natural Light

We stood in the kitchen and the realtor said,
"Isn't this gorgeous? There's so much natural light."
It was, and it is—if gorgeous is sunlight streaming
through smudged-fingerprint windows onto floorboards
covered with something sticky and crumbs no matter
how many times we sweep. What I pictured then: you
and me sipping coffee while the children play and we
can talk. What it is: you and me telling the children
"let her have a turn" while our coffee gets cold. How
many times will we catch each other's eye thinking,
this is what they say we'll miss? But smiling half a
second later because we know it's true. Even as I go
to clean the windows my heart skips a beat—for the
way their handprints will never be this small again,
as soon as tomorrow, and that there will come a day
when they won't run to the window to watch the rain
fall, telling us to come look, and we do—but at them,
our daughters, too good to be true. Isn't it gorgeous?
Just look at their natural light.

```
   Isn't
         it
             something
how                              you

can
  let

this

                         be



              good
```

These Years, These Days

How will I explain these years of my life?
The years gone by in days like this—
following her around the park
keeping mulch out of her mouth
and when she gets tired
carrying her back to the car
or to sit on a bench
where she rests her head on my shoulder
and points out all the birds
and planes.
How will I explain?
Only to say that
years from now
I will be walking in this park
and just the sight of this bench
will make me ache.

Cautionary Tales

Someday you will hear the story of a rainbow fish
who did not have friends
until she made herself fit in.
My child,
you do not have to lose your sparkle
for others to shine
and if this feels true?
Keep swimming.

Someday you will hear the story of a giving tree
who harmed itself
until there was nothing left.
My child,
you do not have to make yourself smaller
for others to grow
and if this feels true?
Stay rooted.

Someday you will hear the story of a mother
who drives across town with a ladder
strapped to her car.
My child,
you do not have to bear the burden of another's love
that refuses to change shape
and if this feels true?
Let go.

These are the stories I heard
when I was a child
and what they taught me
was this:
what matters most is
not the stories we're told
but the stories
we tell ourselves.

What I Want to Tell My Daughter When She Falls Over and Over as She Learns to Walk

This is a feeling you might never outgrow.
Just this morning, that same old heartbreak
I thought I had figured out back then–
the way the world and my body in it
can still feel so heavy–
and yet
I got out of bed
watched the sun come up
and listened to the birds sing
with your sister in my arms.
All of this is to say
when the baby book
asks about your first steps
I want you to keep in mind:
this is when you learned to get back up.

The Way With Children

an afternoon goes by—
chasing houseflies
pitting cherries
watching the ceiling fan turn—
little nuisances
little marvels.

Ode to Mary Oliver

To be a mother of young children
you must pay attention
I do not mean when you feel like it
I mean every single moment
quite seriously
this is life or death
(just now in writing this down
my daughter wandered into the yard
where I know
a wasp nest awaits—
but before she reaches it
before I reach her
she bends to examine
the most tender blade of grass
and holds it out to me like a miracle
and it is)
where was I?
Let me begin again—
this, too, is how it goes—
being a mother of small children
has made me realize
what has always been true:
you must pay attention
this is life.

Happy (and She Knows It)

Sometimes my baby claps so hard
or hugs her teddy bear
so tightly
she
falls
down
right on the spot
this kind of exuberance
knocks her off her feet—literally.
True, someday she won't be
quite so topsy-turvy
but I hope the balance
of her life
always
        leans
                toward
                        joy.

Car Nap

You don't know
this wasn't the plan
you just let your tired be tired
and shouldn't it be?
What if every love on earth
was as simple as this—
so safe you could fall asleep in it
knowing wherever we go
you are close
to home.

Looking at Her Looking at Me

My child tells me to "watch this"
all day long
I am in the middle of something
and she is in the middle of something
that needs to be seen
so I stop what I'm doing
and see her
but the face she makes
as she concentrates
and the way she sits
with one leg tucked beneath
make it clear
she is the one
who has been watching me.

I'll Be Down Soon

We tuck the children into bed
and meet halfway down the hall
there's not much time before we hear
one of them start to call
"I've got this," you say, "I'll be down soon"
and we smile as if it's true
but these days it's a coin toss
as to whether you will
or I'll still be awake
by the time you do
so I get the monitor and listen
as you sing her to sleep
all the while knowing
there will come a time
when it's just you and me
and the little ones who need us now
won't sleep under our roof
and though it seems so far away
I know when that day comes, we'll say
I guess we meant it after all
here we are
so soon.

The Butterfly Effect

Our daughter wraps the blanket
around her shoulders
pretends to be
a butterfly
a delicate thing
how I once turned left
(I could have turned right)
onto his street.

Laundry List

To never be done—
in this am talking about
mothering
as well as laundry
which waits for me
between cycles and seasons
in baskets where the children sit
too big for the clothes they wore last week
too young to remember any of this
but someday
the feeling of warm towels
around their shoulders
might remind them
of me.

To My Secondborn

Before you were born
everyone said so many things
mostly, "You won't believe
how much your heart can love"
but I sort of believed it right away
and definitely believed it
the moment I held you

What they should've been saying
what I really can't believe even now
is how much I can do
with one hand—
brush teeth, make coffee,
get the mail, start the laundry—
and that's just the first hour of today

I admit when I hold you
I am usually doing something else
or thinking about something else
this time around there is
less gazing into each other's eyes
more measuring of mess
but listen—

with your sister,
life became
a song
and with you in my arms
as we go about our days
life has become
a dance.

Idea

What if we stop
telling our daughters
to use their inside voices
whenever we mean quiet
what if they grow up knowing
the voice inside of them
should always be
loudest of all.

A Mom on Social Media

Everyone else potty trained at age two in two days.
Try these fifty-eight lunch ideas for toddlers in rainbow colors and fun shapes. Parents today are too soft /
too hard / too there / too not there. Why you should
only have one child, why you should have more than
one child, why more people than ever are choosing to
be child-free. The best age gap for sibling relationships.
Pacifier-use past the age of three causes developmental
delays. Taking turns vs. sharing. Why you shouldn't say
"be careful." Homeschool / public school / private school
is the best option. I could never be a stay-at-home mom.
I could never work when they are young. I could never
do it without my village. I cannot afford the village.
Funny video about moms' night out, mom math, mom
wearing sweatpants while her child goes around in a
princess dress. Majority of kids are not kindergarten-
ready. Important sleep habits for early brain development.
Favorite Montessori activities for a six-month-old. How to
say goodbye. How to tell if your child is securely attached.
Show me more.
Show me more.

you

are

the

best

mom

for

your child

Beach Body

I still think of
the way we were as girls
lying in the shallow end
bellies rising above the water
calling ourselves
an island.

My Daughter's Hunger
(Part II)

She awakens in a field of strawberries
picks them as fast as she can eat
even the stems
before I can tell her not to.
On the way: visions of pies
and jams to last all winter
gone as I watch her
shirt stain red
sticky hands, chin, hair
while the box for gathering
remains bare.
I thought I would teach her
what it means to wait, but
there is a field of strawberries at her feet
and she is not concerned
with what's to come.
There is a lesson in this too.

Laws of Nature

I ask how you slept even though you always say good, even in the
newborn days when it really pissed me off to hear you say good

thousands of mornings together and I still want to know
or maybe that's giving myself too much credit

maybe I ask because it's a habit, the way love over time
often becomes, the way I feared it would before all of this began.

I would look at the way we kiss now when leaving or returning—
sometimes on the lips but often on the forehead or cheek

as I turn to pour coffee or check on the children—
and see something ordinary. And it is

as ordinary as the way the tide reaches for the shore
and the rhythm of a whole universe goes on.

Here we are coming home to each other, and it is not habit
but gravity between us.

Spoilers

The magnolia in the backyard isn't dead
someday your baby will sleep through the night
and so will you
your hair will grow back
and you will stop caring about stretch marks
they won't always take turns but
her favorite word will be her sister's name
he will buy you flowers for no reason
and you will get butterflies again
you will keep at it
even after all this time
like you're just getting started
it takes a magnolia ten years to bloom.

To a Dear Friend

May you eat more than their crumbs
while standing at the counter
and pray for more
than another blessed minute of sleep
more than anything
may you love yourself so much
you do not have to cross the ocean
to find her
just look how far
you've already come.

Tiny Universe

I wanted to know which planet shone
outside the window where I stood
while the coffee brewed
I would have to look it up later—
my children were waking
and the coffee was nearly done
but when I picked up my pen
to make note of it
I started a grocery list instead
the apple bowl sat empty in front of me
and the girls would be asking for them
sliced in the shapes of things like stars
here was the universe
and my place in it
let me be clear:
it was as bright if not more so
and I was no less amazed.

Mindfulness

If you think about it blowing bubbles is just
a breathing exercise with flair. Turns out you
exhale longer than inhale when you must make
enough bubbles for both children to pop. What
motherhood has shown me: mindfulness comes
in the most unexpected ways—like when I count
to ten while she hides in the curtains, or count to
three so slowly in hopes she'll listen to what I say
(and accept she probably won't). How many broken
pieces will I glue back together, telling myself that's
how the light gets in? And through everything, this
constant chant of "mom mom mommy" in case I
could forget—there is only ever the present moment,
with all its pressing needs. Another snack, another
boo-boo, another pair of sticky hands that reach to
be wiped or held. This endless body scanning for
what aches or to memorize what's there before they
grow up even more. Just yesterday she was a baby,
and if I blink, she will get on a school bus. Lest I lose
myself inside these thoughts, my daughter tugs me
back to what's here: a change in the light, half-moon
in blue sky, dust motes between her and me. So often
being a mother is learning just to be.

you

                                     must

    accept

                                        everything

                 will

                     change

Instructions for Calming Down

Closed my eyes
held her hand
would know it was hers
anywhere
and could feel
how small it was
in mine.

Doing My Best

Lately I'm always running late
or falling behind
and everywhere I go
I'm holding up the line
as I dig through my diaper bag
for a wallet I can't find
balancing a baby on my hip
where she leaves a patch of drool
on my side
but the reason I'm late
is because when my toddler asked
for one more story I said yes
and I could've changed my shirt
but instead I embraced the mess
there will always be more
I should be doing
but time with them is less and less
and these days I'm learning
to let go of the rest
so the next time
you look at a mother
I hope you see a woman
doing her best.

Core Memory

Sometimes I wake in the night
and still feel her kick
near that little divot
where muscles split
beneath my belly button
that once was the receiving end
of a love that doesn't quit
too young to remember, and so is she
but this is deeper than memory–
this is what we're made of.

As for Me and My House

We will not let dishes stand in the way
of an after-dinner dance party.
Our piles of books will be as tall as the laundry
so that neither will ever be done.
There will be muddy boots by the door
and windows smudged by sticky hands
that pointed out the moon and stars.
Mess and wonder will always be welcome here
and we will light up every time a child walks in the room
even in the middle of the night
so wherever they go, they know
home is the feeling of being seen.

Soundtrack

White noise / little footsteps running
down the hall / laughing / crying / running
water that sounds like crying / You Are My
Sunshine / peekaboo / birdsong / the coffee
pot / the bottle warmer / the washing machine /
train whistles / "mama" / mommy always
comes back / blowing noses and kisses /
splash / pop! / *Goodnight Moon* / watch
this / gentle / take turns / take your
time / the ticking of a clock / more,
more / all done.

Little Shoes

When the day is done
I sweep the crumbs
and line their shoes up
one by one
I wash the baby spoons
in the sink
start the laundry
and try not to think
about how someday the cups
won't all have lids
and none of the bedrooms
will have a crib
and what I would give then
for one more day
when little shoes lined
the entryway.

Buckling My Toddler Into Her Car Seat

I wish she wouldn't
kick her feet
when I buckle her
into her car seat
but when did her legs
get so strong?
I still remember
the first time
we drove her home.

When the News Is Terrible Again

I cannot fix the world, but I can fix her another sandwich when hers is cut in half and she wanted it whole. I can kiss scraped knees, rebuild the Lego tower that got knocked over, tape the pages of her favorite book that are torn from use. What if all this adds up to another person who grows up to have her heart broken? But who knows when it does that we must do what we can to put things back together again. Maybe this is how you change the world after all.

A Magic Trick

If I blink
she will grow
or else
she will disappear
even now it seems
easy to believe
I dreamt it all.

While You Are Reading This

Chances are you'll think about what to make for dinner, the load of laundry that needs to be folded, or the paper you still need to sign in her backpack. Maybe this is the moment you recognize how thirsty you are or finally answer the group text about why you can't come to the birthday party during nap time. Quick flash of dread about the way the world is turning. Quick flash of awe at the way the world keeps turning. A softening as light as the indent of the dimples on the back of the baby's knuckles as you held her hand through midnights, through the bars of the crib. And just this note to remind you how amazing it is that in each moment you hold space

for them

        and for all of it.

This Never Gets Old

I wake to the sound of her singing
through the monitor
and when I walk into her room
she reaches up for me
tucks her head between my neck and shoulder
and tells me about her dreams–
this never gets old
but she will

These days she doesn't walk
she runs or skips or spins
and when a song starts playing
she stops wherever we are
and asks
if we can dance–
this never gets old
but she will

When she falls down
she still wants me to kiss her knees
and when she does something new
I'm the first to see.
At night, when I tuck her in,
she always wants one more story–
this never gets old
but she will

I know there will come a day
without the monitor by my bed
and even if it were, my arms would be
too tired to pick up this little girl
for she's not the only one getting older
I'm getting older too
and when that day comes
I'll look back in gratitude

She may call me "mom"
instead of "mommy" then
I just hope that she still calls
so I can thank her
for the time of my life
and smile lines on my face
from these years
when she was small.

If the World Ended Tomorrow

I would spend today with my children
sitting at the breakfast table, talking about
their dreams, listening to them argue and
laugh and cry without regard for time the
way children have since the beginning
and will until the end. If it were winter,
we would go outside and catch snowflakes
on our tongues. If it were spring, we would
go outside and make wishes on dandelions.
I would wish for what I always do: more
time. They would wish for what they always
do: pizza. We would have pizza and I would
burn my mouth because I never did learn.
In the bath, I'd use all the bubbles and catch
myself counting down to bedtime until I
remembered. Later, I would watch them sleep.
It would be like any other day. In the end,
all I ever wanted was this.

Notes

"An infant's first breath . . . inflates the lungs . . . dramatically decreases lung pressure and resistance to blood flow, causing a major circulatory reconfiguration" source: courses.lumenlearning.com/suny-ap2/chapter/adjustments-of-the-infant-at-birth-and-postnatal-stages/#:~:text=The%20first%20breath%20typically%20is,causing%20a%20major%20circulatory%20reconfiguration.

About the Author

Rachel Beachy lives in Kentucky with her husband and children. She writes at her kitchen table. This is her first collection of poetry.

www.ingramcontent.com/pod-product-compliance
Lightning Source LLC
Chambersburg PA
CBHW030908170426
43193CB00009BA/778